BEAUTIFUL Wreaths

Walter B. Fedyshyn, AIFD, PFCI

Kay Brandau Hood, AIFD

Alan and Virginia Preston

Karen Almy Stovall

Publications International, Ltd.

Contributing Writers and Wreath Designers:
Walter B. Fedyshyn, **AIFD, PFCI,** is a member of the American Institute of Floral Designers (AIFD) and the Professional Floral Commentators International (PFCI). His floral designs have been published in design books and national trade magazines including *Professional Floral Designer, Florist Review,* and *Flowers &.* He is also a featured columnist for *Floral & Nursery Times.* Walter is the co-owner of Zuverink Fine Silk Botanicals.

Kay Brandau Hood, AIFD, is a member of the American Institute of Floral Designers (AIFD). She owns her own design studio, K. Brandau Designs, where she specializes in custom silk designs for homes and offices. Kay also teaches design to both beginning and advanced students.

Alan and Virginia Preston are floral designers who have been making preserved botanical arrangements since 1986. Their designs are available in over 450 stores nationally, through large catalog companies, and on their website: www.vpreston.com.

Karen Almy Stovall is a full-time floral designer with a degree from the Corcoran School of Art in Washington, D.C., and she has had private schooling in the art of Ichibana floral arranging. She works at Fort Valley Nursery, a full-scale gardening, home, and landscaping center, where she designs and creates wreaths, swags, centerpieces, and commissioned projects using dried, silk, or fresh materials.

Illustrations by Denise Hilton Campbell

Photography by Silver Lining Digital, Inc.

Photo Styling by Lisa Wright

Copyright © 2002 Publications International, Ltd. All rights reserved. This book may not be reproduced or quoted in whole or in part by any means whatsoever without written permission from:

Louis Weber, CEO
Publications International, Ltd.
7373 North Cicero Avenue
Lincolnwood, Illinois 60712

Permission is never granted for commercial purposes.

Manufactured in China.

8 7 6 5 4 3 2 1

ISBN: 0-7853-6009-3

contents

4	making beautiful wreaths
12	gilded harvest
14	gardener's delight
16	pinecone and twig
18	spring fresh florals
20	southern magnolia holiday
22	fore!
24	country kitchen
26	traditional christmas
28	nautical notions
30	earthy autumn swag
32	rain forest square
34	candy-coated christmas
36	autumn berry candle rings
38	birdhouse bounty
40	holiday pear garland
42	high style fall
44	sunflower garden
46	autumn splendor
48	rose hydrangea
50	four calling birds
52	summer eucalyptus
54	halloween spooktacular
56	new england holiday
58	victorian valentine heart
60	williamsburg medallion
62	stars and stripes forever

page 42

page 28

page 34

making beautiful wreaths

For years, the wreath has been a lasting symbol of celebration and love. For many holidays and many special occasions, a beautiful wreath is a perfect decoration. Wreaths help us celebrate holidays including Christmas, Halloween, and the Fourth of July, just to name a few. They help us welcome spring, summer, fall, and winter. Even birthdays, anniversaries, and weddings can be made more fun and festive with a wreath. And, maybe most important, a wreath greets guests at our front door and makes the inside of our home even warmer and more inviting.

In this beautifully photographed book, you'll find wonderful wreaths you can make yourself. With clear, step-by-step instructions, you'll be amazed at your results. And once you've mastered the basics, you'll be able to add your own personal touches to make the designs all your own.

This introduction is packed with important information that will help you in the construction of your wreath. Check out the descriptive list of basic tools and supplies you'll need. Valuable information is also included on selecting the proper wreath bases and forms. The segment on "Designing Tips" will give you ideas and suggestions to help stimulate your own creative juices.

Remember that practice makes perfect, so take your time and enjoy yourself! Read through the instructions, then gather your materials and begin. You'll soon be creating your own beautiful wreaths!

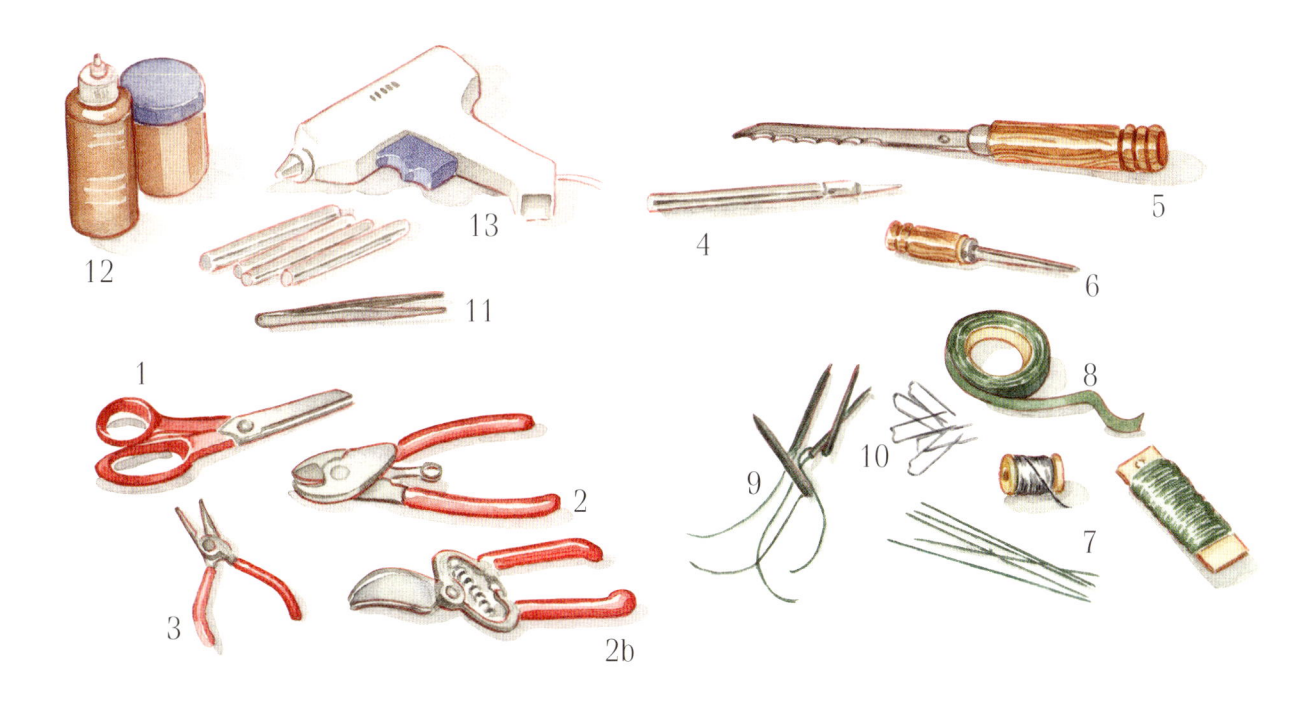

Tools and Floral Supplies

You should have these basic tools and supplies on hand as you begin to make wreaths. Become familiar with them. Some tools you may already own, while others you may have to buy. They should be available at craft and hobby stores as well as from local hardware stores.

1. Scissors should be sharp. Fabric scissors will be used for cutting ribbons and fabrics. Keep them handy; you will reach for them often. Also keep on hand a pair of heavy-duty scissors for cutting other items, such as florals, thin wire, or other craft items. Don't mix up the scissors—use the fabric scissors on fabric only to keep them sharp.

2. Wire cutters are for cutting silk flower stems, floral wire, and other objects that cannot be cut by scissors. Wire cutter can also be used to cut small branches and stems of dried flowers. Garden clippers (see 2b) are also useful to have on hand for clipping heavier branches and stems.

3. Needle-nosed pliers are used to grasp materials that your fingers cannot. They are also helpful when twisting heavier gauge wire. This is an all-purpose tool.

4. A small craft knife is not an essential tool, but it can come in handy. Use it in place of scissors to cut materials such as corrugated cardboard.

5. A serrated knife, or a steak knife, is used to cut and shape floral and plastic foam.

6. An awl resembles an ice pick and can be used to make a hole in a straw wreath or into artificial fruit that requires the attachment of a wooden pick.

7. Floral wire comes in many gauges. The higher the gauge number, the finer the wire. You'll use 16-gauge wire to make a hanger for your wreath, while you'll want to use finer wire (18- and 20-gauge wire) for strengthening flower stems. The

finer gauges can be used when you are making bows. Wire is sold in straight lengths as well on spools and paddles. If it is to be used for stems, straight lengths are best. Wrap the finer spool or paddle wire around clusters or groupings of smaller materials when attaching them to a wreath or garland.

8. Floral tape is a waxy crepe paper that will stick only to itself when stretched. It is available in many colors. Choose the shade closest to the materials you are working with (you may need several different colors for the same wreath), and use it to cover stems and to reinforce wire floral picks.

9. Wired floral picks are made of wood and come in several lengths. Use them to reinforce or lengthen stems that you will insert in floral or plastic foam or into a straw wreath.

10. Greening, or fern pins, are U-shaped pins. They are also known as pole, craft, or floral pins. Use them to attach materials to foam or straw wreaths.

11. Tweezers are occasionally needed to handle small items, especially when you are working with hot glue.

12. Craft glues range in consistency from thick to thin. You usually have to wait between steps for the glue to dry. Always have some on hand and select ones that dry clear. Bottled glues are thinner, while the round "pots" of glue are thicker and tackier.

13. Glue guns are one of the most timesaving of all craft tools. There are guns for hot glue, low-temperature glue, and those that dispense either type at the flip of the switch. There is no need to wait between steps because the glue sets up in seconds. NOTE: When selecting a gun that requires its own special glue, be sure you have a source for buying additional glue.

Hot glue guns melt glue at 380 degrees, and glue that hot can cause severe burns. They are not recommended for use by children. If used correctly, their advantages far outweigh this one disadvantage.

Low-temperature glue guns dispense glue at a much lower temperature. The chances of being burned are less—though children should still be supervised when using a low-temp glue gun. If you've used a low-temp gun, avoid hanging your wreaths outdoors where the hot sun could melt the glue, which will loosen the materials. Low-temperature glue is ideal for indoor use, and it can be used on plastic and floral foam without melting it.

Regardless of which glue gun you use, work quickly once you have applied the melted glue. The glue loses its adhesiveness as it cools. Hold the glued object in place for a few seconds while the glue cools.

When you're done gluing, you may find many fine webs of glue hanging from your completed wreath. Use tweezers to remove them from fragile dried materials. If you find them in a wreath made with sturdier materials, such as a pinecone wreath, use a hand-held hair dryer to melt them away.

Wreath Bases

Now that you have gathered your tools, you are ready to select materials to complete your design. Choosing the wreath base will be one decision to make. When determining the size, remember that the larger the base, the more materials and time will be required to complete it. Also, keep proportion in mind. Large flowers, for example, are not appropriate when placed on a tiny wreath, and small items may be lost on a large wreath. The choices of wreath bases are many, and each type offers a variety of shapes. From circles to hearts, to swags, to crescents, these bases will often dictate the type of design.

Straw wreaths

and those made of grapevines or twigs are attractive and very popular. When left partially exposed, the grapevine and twigs add interesting texture to the design.

Honeysuckle wreaths

work well, and, like grapevine wreaths, are available in a multitude of sizes. A thinner, softer version of the grapevine, honeysuckle wreaths are perfect for small, delicate designs.

Eucalyptus wreaths,

with the leaves either dried or made from silk or plastic, are available in many sizes.

Foam wreaths

are lightweight, but they must be covered by ribbon or other materials before decorating. They don't last as long as some other forms, but they are easy to work with. They also come in a variety of shapes.

Premade silk foliage wreaths

are also easy to use. Look for premade evergreen, ivy, magnolia, or lemon leaf wreaths. Just add silk flowers and ribbons for a quick wreath.

Wire wreath forms

are for those who really want to construct their own wreath—from the bottom up. These forms are used to make your own wreath—you add whatever florals or silks to create exactly the look you want.

Ribbon

Ribbon plays an important role in wreath design. When selecting ribbon for your project, think about the theme and style you are trying to accomplish in your wreath. An informal wreath should sport a casual ribbon, while a more sophisticated wreath will be enhanced by something elegant. Choose colors and styles to complement your home décor.

Ribbons are sold in many widths, and using more than one width of coordinated ribbons on the same wreath will add a lovely accent.

Ribbons range from velvet and polyester to cotton and satin. For an elegant touch, consider using metallic tones or any of the new sheer ribbons that are popular today. Wire-edge ribbons allow you to shape your bows in a unique fashion. Be careful though—too many oversized ribbons or bows will overpower your wreath.

New and exciting ribbons are constantly being introduced. With all of these choices it becomes a challenge to select your favorite. Let your imagination lead you.

Natural Materials

There are countless varieties of natural materials on the market that will highlight a wreath or become a major part of the design. A Christmas wreath may be highlighted with cones, while an herb wreath is made up of preserved or dried materials.

Materials that are air dried or dried with desiccant, such as silica gel, are more brittle and will shed. There are spray sealers available to help preserve their natural beauty. Materials preserved with glycerin are soft and pliable and remain so indefinitely.

Don't overlook the texture and beauty of mosses when designing your wreath. Whether you cover the entire wreath or glue tiny accent pieces at random, the design is enhanced by its use. Spanish moss, found hanging from trees in the southern United States and in tropical America, is a light feathery gray moss commonly used in making wreaths. Commercially processed, it is free of insects. Lovely green mosses, such as sheet moss and sphagnum, will add texture and color to your wreath.

Don't forget the versatility of cones and pods, whether you make an entire wreath of them or use them as embellishments. They can be wired into clusters and then wired onto a wreath frame. They can also be hot glued to straw or grapevine wreath forms. The texture of the pods and cones makes an exciting wreath design for fall and winter decorating.

How-to Floral Procedures

This section explains how to perform several of the steps necessary to complete designs in this book.

Hanging a Wreath

Chenille stem hanger: Use only on wreaths covered with materials that will conceal this hanger. Bend a 12-inch length evenly into a U. Twist the U end into a 1- or 2-inch oval loop. Wrap and twist the ends around the wreath tightly, positioning the loop at the top. Apply hot glue to twisted end to reinforce.

VARIATION: Use the same technique to wrap the chenille stem tightly around a wire wreath form or a grapevine wreath, placing it far enough down the back so it is not visible from the front. You can wrap the chenille stem with floral tape so it is easier to hide. You can also use a length of a medium-weight wire taped with floral tape. Covering a wire hanger with floral tape will help prevent scratch marks on the door or wall.

Wire loop hanger: Use only on straw or plastic foam wreaths. Bend 6 inches of heavy floral wire into a U. Twist the U end into a 1-inch oval loop. Bend the cut ends at right angles to the loop and push into the foam or straw until the loop is flush with the wreath. Secure to the wreath with hot glue placed on the bent end of the hanger.

In most cases, you will add the hanger to the wreath frame before you add the materials. Make sure the hook is on the back of the wreath, and be sure the wreath hangs flat on your door or wall before continuing with the wreath. It's harder to fix any problems after the wreath has been assembled.

Floral Tape

Floral tape will stick only to itself when stretched. To apply, break off a length or hook the tape over your little finger. Stretch and wrap the tape around the stem diagonally. Overlap the tape, allowing it to stick to itself, and break it off at the end.

Floral Picks

Use wired floral picks to lengthen or strengthen weak stems before inserting them into plastic foam, floral foam, or straw. Attach the picks by overlapping the wired end of the pick with about 1 inch of the stem end. Spiral wrap the wire tightly around both, working down 1 inch. Continue wrapping one time around the pick itself, and then back up with the rest of the wire. This helps lock the two together.

Multiloop Bow

1. Unroll several yards from a bolt of ribbon. Form loops of ribbon with your dominant hand. Pinch the center of the loops with the thumb and forefinger of your other hand as you work.

2. Continue to add loops to your bow. Keep pinching the bow's center with your thumb and forefinger. After you have all the loops you need, trim away excess ribbon from the bolt. If you want a streamer, leave the ribbon longer before cutting.

3. Insert a length of wire around the center of the ribbon. Bring the two wire ends together securely and tightly next to the bow's center to eliminate loop slippage. Attach the bow to the wreath with the wire. You can also trim the wire and glue the bow in place.

Note: When using heavier ribbon, use a chenille stem to secure the bow. The tiny hairs on the stem will hold the bow securely and not allow twisting of the bare wire. For tiny, delicate bows, thin cloth-covered wire can be used for securing. It eliminates slipping and is so tiny that it disappears into the bow loops.

E-Z Bow

1. This bow is added directly to a wreath. Cut the desired number of ribbon lengths to make the streamers. Angle- or V-cut streamer ends. Crimp the streamers in the middle, and attach them to the wreath with a floral pin.

2. Cut the desired number of ribbons to make individual clustered loops; angle- or V-cut the ends of each piece.

   To make a cluster, fold the end of one strip 6 inches with wrong sides together. Crimp the ribbon midway at 3 inches, and continue folding and crimping to the end of the ribbon length. Place a floral pin over the crimped center, and attach it to the wreath above the streamers. Repeat for all ribbons.

3. Place the individual clusters in a tight group. Fluff the loops to conceal the pins.

Designing Tips

The wreaths on the following pages have been created for you to make, and we encourage you to duplicate them. We also urge you to come up with wreath designs of your own. Here are a few suggestions to help stimulate your creativity.

Study pictures of wreaths in books, magazines, and even mail-order catalogs. Decide what you like, don't like, and why. Check out the combinations of colors and how the florals and accessories are arranged. After some practice, you will begin to develop your own sense of style. You will begin to grow and become more experienced in creating your own designs.

As you study different wreaths, notice that your eyes may be drawn to a particular area of interest. This area should be pleasing to look at and convey the message of the theme. This is considered the "focal point" of the wreath. Not all wreaths must have a focal point, but those that do will draw the viewer's attention.

If you can't decide where to start, begin by choosing a theme—a special holiday or season of the year. Another way to get started is to pick your ribbon first. Then you can pick up the ribbon colors in the floral accessories you gather for the wreath. You could take the same approach using silk or dried flowers as your inspiration.

After you have picked your theme and gathered your materials, sketch your design. But don't let your sketch keep you from changing your plans. Once you've begun, allow yourself some flexibility. If the design is not too intricate, lay your materials on the wreath frame but don't glue or attach them. Change the arrangement of the materials until something suits you. Leave it for several hours or overnight. Then study it again as though you were seeing it for the first time. If you don't like something, change it. When satisfied, assemble the wreath permanently.

For the best perspective, always try to arrange your wreath in a hanging position. If that is not possible, view it upright between steps. Study it from a distance, or look at it in a mirror. If the materials are not balanced, appear overpowering, or look crowded, the wreath's reflection will tell you that.

If this is your first experience with making wreaths, you may not be aware of the infinite choices of accessories at your disposal. Visit local flower shops and hobby and craft stores to acquaint yourself with the current market. There are colorful birds, as well as birdhouses, nests, and eggs that all fit in well with spring and summer themes, not to mention fall and Christmas.

Silk or dried flowers, stuffed animals, or even gardening tools can become the focal point of your wreath. Everyday items such as sewing notions, small toys, and stationery supplies can develop into a special theme. Countless varieties of fresh or permanent fruits, vegetables, and berries can form the basis of a culinary wreath.

Use cones or shells that you collected on vacation. Even old greeting cards can become treasured decorations for a holiday wreath. If a design plan does not evolve immediately, do not be discouraged. Keep your goal in mind, and when you least expect it the idea could surface.

We have opened the gate leading to a new and
creative adventure for you. Now, step inside and follow the path
to develop your own personal style of design.
Enjoy your accomplishments!

gilded harvest

A fall wreath of classic eucalyptus is given a regal update with gold gilding. Lush, deep-toned hydrangeas and harvest berry clusters add texture and interest to the rich golden highlights. Use this wreath for both fall and holiday decorating.

What You'll Need

Premade eucalyptus wreath (dried, plastic, or silk), 24 inches

Gold spray paint

7 stems red silk hydrangea

5 berry stems

Wire cutters

Hot glue gun, glue sticks

8 small bunches caspia or statice, dried or silk

1. Spray wreath with gold spray paint. Spray evenly to coat all branches. Let dry overnight.

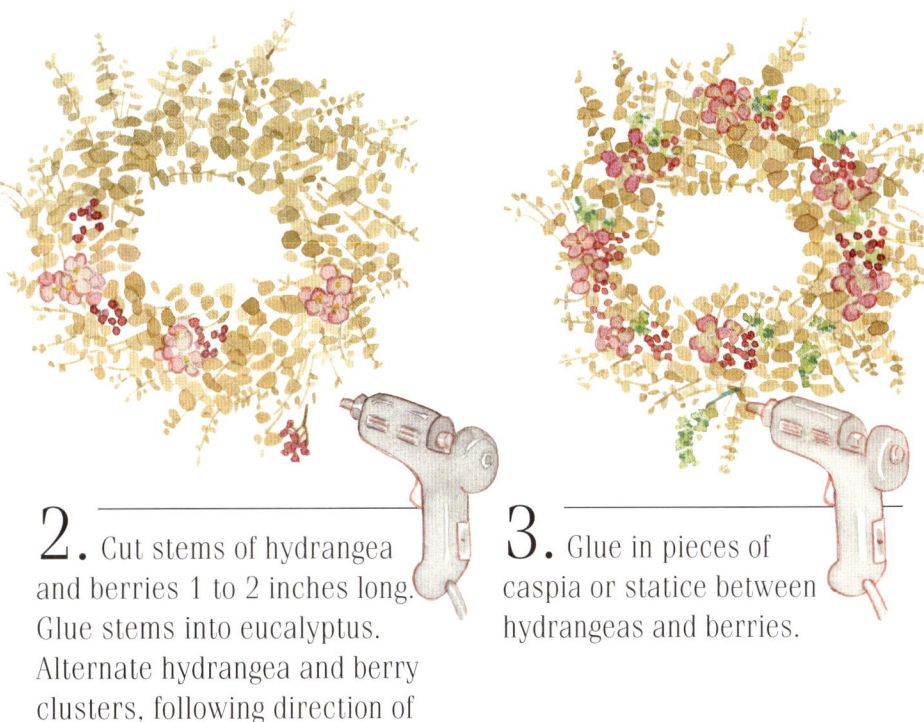

2. Cut stems of hydrangea and berries 1 to 2 inches long. Glue stems into eucalyptus. Alternate hydrangea and berry clusters, following direction of eucalyptus.

3. Glue in pieces of caspia or statice between hydrangeas and berries.

Tip

If you can't find a eucalyptus wreath, wire 5 to 6 stems of eucalyptus into a bunch with floral wire. Each bunch should be 7 to 8 inches long. Make enough bunches to cover wire frame. Wire eucalyptus bunches to frame with small pieces of floral wire. Keep all bunches going in the same direction.

Variations

Add extra highlights by tucking in fall leaves, either silk or dried. For an extra gilded touch, lightly spray leaves with gold paint. Remember to let spray-painted materials dry overnight. Any type of silk or dried fluffy filler materials can be used in place of caspia or statice. Choose materials smaller than the larger hydrangea and berry clusters, which should appear dominant. The trick is to pick materials with different textures so they contrast nicely.

gardener's delight

This garden wreath is a reminder of the smell of fresh soil, unfolding plants, and the coming of spring. You'll smile every time you see your sunny creation.

What You'll Need

Grapevine wreath, 18 inches
Brown chenille stem
Hot glue gun, glue sticks
12 inches brown twine, ⅛ inch wide
2 small sticks, about 1 inch long each
6 clay flowerpots: two 1 inch, two 2 inch, two 3 inch
Floral wire
Wire cutters
Ivy or other cascading green plant
2 small clusters of grapes
Small bird's nest
Small bird
Small plastic eggs
Small bunch white silk flowers
2 miniature garden tools
Sheet moss

1. Twist chenille stem on back of wreath to form a hook for hanging. Glue in place.

2. Tie a loose knot 4 inches from bottom of twine. Slip small stick through knot, tighten knot around stick, and thread a 1-inch pot on twine. Make a second knot about 4 inches above bottom of flowerpot, insert stick, tighten knot around stick, and thread other small flowerpot onto twine. Second pot should overlap top of first pot. Set aside.

3. Glue and wire a 2-inch pot to bottom center of wreath, with pot opening facing down and to the right. Glue the other 2-inch pot to inside of first pot. Glue and wire a 3-inch pot to left of 2-inch pots. This pot should be upright. Glue and wire another 3-inch pot to left of other 3-inch pot, placing this one a step above first.

4. Cut ivy into 10- to 12-inch strands. Glue 3 ivy pieces at base of pots, and gracefully angle them up wreath and to the left. Glue in place. Glue 4 ivy pieces under flowerpots, angling them around 2 small flowerpots. Leave a tail or two hanging down.

5. Wire 1 grape cluster into wreath at 10 o'clock and 1 just below pots at base of wreath. Glue bird's nest below 3-inch pots. Glue bird to edge of nest and eggs in nest.

6. Glue short sprigs of ivy into 3-inch pot at left. Glue white flowers into same pot.

7. Angle a garden tool upright in left-most pot, and glue into place. Place handle of other tool in nest, and glue in place.

8. Tie flowerpots from step 2 to top of wreath. Glue sheet moss to cover any glue or wire that shows.

pinecone and twig

This traditional holiday decoration is rustic and yet so elegant! Every visitor to your home will admire the warm beauty of this stunning wreath.

What You'll Need

Garden clippers
2 pounds of tips from any tree
Wire wreath form,
8 inches
Paddle floral wire,
24 gauge
50 pinecones, various sizes
Bunch of red cannella berries
Bag quince slices
Hot glue gun, glue sticks
2 yards red-and-cream
plaid ribbon

1. Use garden clippers to cut sticks in varying lengths between 4½ and 9 inches long.

2. Attach wire to wreath by wrapping it once around wreath and twisting it on back to secure. (Do not cut wire.)

3. Make a small bunch of 10 to 12 sticks of various lengths. Place the stick ends over where the wire is attached to the wreath. Wrap ends 3 times, moving down length of ends with each wrap. At last wrap, you will be ½ inch from end of sticks. Make sure wire holds them snugly but not so tightly that they are crushed.

4. Make another bunch of sticks, and place it on top of ends of first bunch. As you wrap, the first wrap will hold last ½ inch of first bunch as well as ends of second bunch. Continue making same size bunches and adding them to wreath.

5. To add last bunch, cut off last ½ inch of stick ends. Gently lift first bunch, and slide last bunch under it. Wrap stems of last bunch 3 times to hold in place, but as you wrap, leave second wrap loose enough to pull paddle under so you can tie off and secure last bunch. Cut wire, leaving a tail of 4 inches of wire. Wrap wire around wreath form to secure. Slide end under ties and between stems.

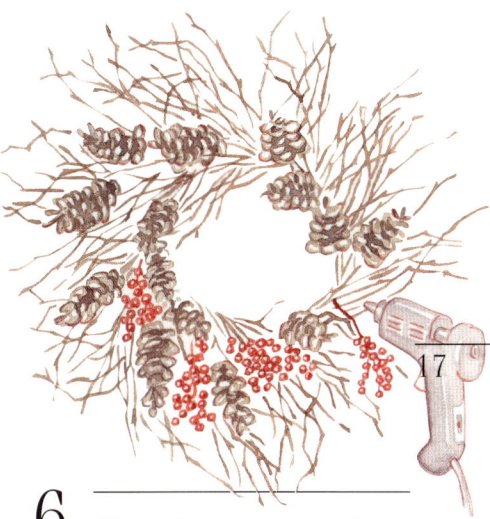

6. Glue pinecones, berries, and quince slices throughout wreath, following direction of sticks.

7. Make bow, and attach it to the 4 o'clock position on wreath with wire.

spring fresh florals

Brightly colored flowers and tender green leaves will lift your spirits each time you look at this carefree arrangement. This wreath will be a reminder of spring's freshness.

What You'll Need

Grapevine wreath, 18 to 20 inches

Brown chenille stem

Hot glue gun, glue sticks

3 large red silk tulips with stems

2 silk forsythia branches with offshoot branches, one 18 inch and one 12 inch

Wire cutters

Floral wire

5 silk fern leaves

Silk ivy trailings

Silk violet bush with leaves

1. Twist chenille stem on back of wreath to form a hook for hanging. Glue in place to secure.

2. Just to right of bottom center of wreath, insert 3 tulips into wreath at different heights. Glue in place.

3. Insert forsythia at base of tulip stems, and bend longer stems gracefully up right side of wreath. Use floral wire to hold forsythia in place. Insert shorter forsythia branch at base of tulips, and bend along bottom of wreath, jutting out to left.

4. Glue 3 fern leaves into a fan shape to left of tulips. Glue 2 fern leaves to right of tulips, and arrange them so they move gracefully up right side of wreath.

5. Cut ivy into 10- to 12-inch lengths, and glue at base of tulip stems. Allow ivy to hang below wreath.

6. Glue violet bush to wreath where tulips, forsythia, and ferns meet. Bend some leaves up and some down.

southern magnolia holiday

The south's most beautiful flower is highlighted on this formal holiday wreath. Elegant ivory magnolias dance through Christmas greenery, glass ornaments, and golden holly leaves.

What You'll Need

Artificial pine wreath
5 silk magnolias with 4 buds
Wire cutters
Floral wire
Hot glue gun, glue sticks
27 gold glass ball ornaments on wire picks, 1 inch each
2 gold silk holly branches
72 inches sheer wired ribbon
10 natural pinecones

1. Cut stems of magnolia flowers to 2 inches. Cut off buds and leaves from stems. Form a collar around flower with leaves, and wrap with floral wire to hold in place. Do the same with buds.

2. Insert magnolias and buds into wreath. Twist pine branches around stems to secure. Add a touch of hot glue for extra security. Space flowers evenly around wreath, leaving room for ornaments.

3. Twist 3 glass balls together to form a cluster. Make 9 clusters. Insert clusters into wreath between magnolias. Twist pine branches around clusters to hold them in place.

4. Cut holly branches into 3- to 4-inch pieces. Glue them into wreath around magnolias. Glue remaining magnolia leaves to hide any wire that shows.

5. Cut ribbon into three 24-inch pieces. Form 2 loops of ribbon, and twist together with floral wire. Secure each ribbon to wreath behind a magnolia. Keep ribbon loops to sides of flowers so flowers remain dominant. Space ribbons evenly around wreath.

6. Glue in pinecones and remaining holly leaves to hide any glue or wire.

Variation

The gold and ivory color combination of this wreath can be changed to suit your home decor. Consider using red, green, or even blue ornaments to complement the classic ivory magnolias. Red and green trim would give the wreath a more traditional appeal for the Christmas season.

fore!

Put your beloved old golf clubs to good use in this fun and creative design. A nest, a golf ball, tees, twigs, and assorted silk flowers are added to complete the look. Surprise a golfing family member or friend with this as a birthday or Christmas gift.

What You'll Need

2 golf clubs
Covered floral wire, 22 gauge
Wire cutters
Pen or pencil
Hot glue gun, glue sticks
2 dried shelf mushrooms on wire stems, 4 to 5 inches wide
Twig bird's nest, 4 inches
Golf ball
2 tees
Stem branched teal berries or spikes, about 10 clusters
Stem burgundy hydrangea or lilac
Stem cream berry clusters
Pliable twigs, 10 to 12 inches long (grapevine, honeysuckle, nito vine, etc.)
Spanish moss

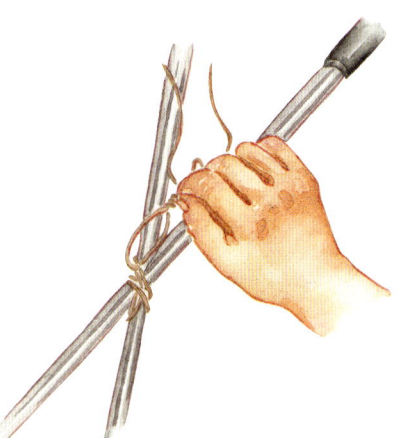

1. Cross golf clubs, and wire them securely together. Twist wire at back of clubs twice, then cross wire ends and twist 3 times, forming a 2-inch loop for the hanger. Curl ends of wire with a pen or pencil. Glue heavily where clubs cross, being careful not to glue the hanging loop. Let glue dry thoroughly.

2. Cut mushroom stems to 2 inches and bend at right angles to mushroom. Place 1 mushroom to the right of junction of clubs and the other slightly below it to the left. Glue stems and base of mushroom to clubs. Secure with another wire.

3. Glue nest to middle of mushrooms, centering it at the junction of the clubs.

4. Glue golf ball into nest, and glue tees into top of nest above ball.

5. Cut teal berries into sections. Glue 5 pieces in a staggered line extending below mushrooms. Glue 3 pieces staggered at top of design above nest. Glue 2 pieces to the left of nest on top of mushrooms.

6. Cut hydrangea into 5 clusters. Glue 1 above nest, 2 to left of nest, 1 directly below bottom mushroom, and last just below that.

7. Cut cream berries into 5 or 6 clusters. Add 1 long cluster to left of teal berries, add another cluster to upper left of nest, add 3 more clusters around nest and mushrooms, and add longest cluster below bottom mushroom. Tuck twig scraps into flowers below nest, extending out and downward. Add a thin cluster of twigs going upward from nest.

8. Turn design over, and glue Spanish moss to cover glue.

country kitchen

Add a bit of cooking whimsy to brighten your kitchen!
For a more rustic look, use antique cookie cutters you find at
a flea market, or substitute the cookie cutters for something else
that reflects your decorating tastes.

What You'll Need

Grapevine wreath, 18 inches
Brown chenille stem
Hot glue gun, glue sticks
Water-soluble matte varnish
Paintbrush
5 small baskets
Floral wire, 24 gauge
Wire cutters
3 large cookie cutters
Cinnamon sticks
2 miniature kitchen tools
A few of each: small plastic eggs, small pretzels, teddy bear graham crackers, bread sticks, small plastic cherries, berry pick
2 wooden spoons
2 yards country-plaid ribbon, 2 inches wide
Scissors

1. Twist chenille stem around back of wreath to form a hook for hanging. Add hot glue to hold hook in place. Brush front of wreath with varnish. Let dry completely.

2. Place baskets on wreath, some leaning in and some leaning out. Wire baskets in place.

3. Wire cookie cutters around inside of wreath. Wire 2 or 3 cinnamon sticks together into bundles; make 5 bundles. Glue a bundle near each cookie cutter. Glue a bundle of cinnamon into each of 2 baskets.

4. Wire a miniature tool to wreath and the other into a basket with cinnamon sticks. Glue eggs, pretzels, graham crackers, bread sticks, cherries, and berries into other baskets.

5. Wire spoons to bottom of wreath. Glue a few cinnamon sticks to wreath jutting out from spoons. Cut 3 inches from ribbon. From small ribbon piece, cut small strips. Tie small bows to a few basket tops and around the cinnamon bundles.

6. With long ribbon piece, make a large multiloop bow and wire it to top of spoons.

traditional christmas

Let the festivities begin! This wreath extends a rich and abundant welcome to all who pass by. The luxuriant colors and fullness spread good cheer.

What You'll Need

Evergreen wreath, 24 inches
16 to 18 silk magnolia leaves,
4 to 6 inches long
Hot glue gun, glue sticks
14 medium pieces of
2-inch wax or plastic fruit:
3 red apples, 4 green apples,
3 pomegranates, 4 lemons
7 small pieces of 1-inch wax
or plastic fruit: 3 pears,
4 pomegranates
8 to 10 pinecones, 2 to 3
inches each
3 yards red velvet ribbon, #40
Scissors
Floral wire, 24 gauge
Wire cutters

1. With wreath on table, fluff branches to create fullness.

2. Glue magnolia leaves around wreath, overlapping them and leaving 4 to 5 inches open at bottom for a bow. Ends of leaves should extend beyond evergreen boughs.

3. Evenly space 3 red apples on wreath at top center, lower left, and lower right, leaving space at wreath bottom for bow. Do not glue yet.

4. Place rest of medium-size fruit around wreath in a pleasing arrangement, with an eye to symmetry. When fruit is in place, glue to wreath.

5. Glue pinecones and small fruit throughout wreath to fill gaps.

6. Using red ribbon, make a multiloop bow with 12-inch tails. Cut ribbon ends on an angle. Wire bow to bottom of wreath.

nautical notions

Feel the calm of a sunny day on the shore and the excitement of finding a shell or starfish hidden in the folds of sea grass with this beautiful wreath. It brings a breath of clean, sea air inside!

What You'll Need

Wire wreath form, 8 inches
Paddle floral wire, 22 gauge
Garden clippers
Bunch preserved, dyed green eucalyptus
Bunch preserved, dyed green lemon leaves
Bunch preserved, dyed green bear grass
Bunch preseved ferns
Hot glue gun, glue sticks
3 to 5 medium sand dollars
3 to 5 medium white starfish
3 to 5 medium seashells
Bunch red statice
Bunch dark blue larkspur

1. Attach wire to back of wreath by wrapping it once around wreath form and twisting it on back to secure. (Do not cut wire.)

2. Cut eucalyptus and lemon leaves 4 to 6 inches long. Cut bear grass 10 to 12 inches long.

3. Make a bouquet of 4 eucalyptus pieces, 2 lemon leaf pieces, and 2 or 3 blades of bear grass. Place stems on wreath where wire is attached. Wrap stems 3 times, moving down length of stems with each wrap. At last wrap, you will be ½ inch from end of stems. Make sure wire holds stems snugly but not so tightly that they are crushed.

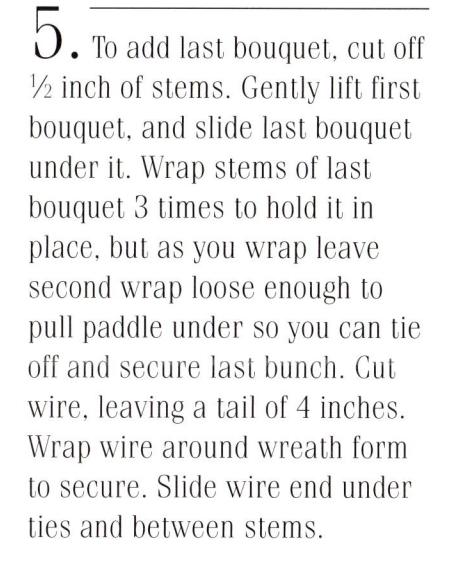

4. Make another bouquet. Place this bouquet on top of stems of first. As you wrap wire, the first wrap will hold last ½ inch of first bouquet as well as top of stems of second bouquet. Continue making bouquets and adding them to wreath. You will need to add about 20 bouquets to cover wreath.

5. To add last bouquet, cut off ½ inch of stems. Gently lift first bouquet, and slide last bouquet under it. Wrap stems of last bouquet 3 times to hold it in place, but as you wrap leave second wrap loose enough to pull paddle under so you can tie off and secure last bunch. Cut wire, leaving a tail of 4 inches. Wrap wire around wreath form to secure. Slide wire end under ties and between stems.

6. Glue ferns throughout wreath, but place the underside of the fern face up. The whiter side gives wreath a more sand-washed appearance.

7. Glue sand dollars, starfish, and seashells throughout wreath. Be sure they are nicely spaced.

8. Glue statice and larkspur throughout wreath. You can also glue in some longer strands of bear grass.

earthy autumn swag

Faux mushrooms and gourds seem to magically sprout among moss, dried fall leaves, and pinecones on a bundle of natural birch branches. Delicate bittersweet vines add rich fall color and texture to this easy-to-make autumn swag.

What You'll Need

Floral wire, 24 gauge
Brown floral tape
Birch branches
2 stems artificial or dried bittersweet
3 artificial mushrooms
2 artificial gourds
3 assorted pinecones
Dried fall leaves
Natural green sheet moss
Hot glue gun, glue sticks

1. Wrap floral wire with brown floral tape. Making sure all branches are going in the same direction, tightly tie bundle of branches together with taped wire about 3 inches from top of bundle. Form a hook with the wire on back of branches so they hang vertically.

2. Wire bittersweet vines to sides of bundle. Place 1 stem on right and 1 stem on left of bundle. Make sure stems of bittersweet are tied into bundle so bittersweet hangs vertically.

3. Glue mushrooms, gourds, and pinecones to birch bundle. Glue in leaves and pieces of moss to hold materials in place as well as to hide glue and wire.

4. Bend bittersweet branches up and over cluster of mushrooms and gourds for movement.

Variations

This beautiful swag could also be used as a dining table centerpiece. The long, low shape lends itself perfectly for the center of the table. Add taper candles and a few votives for an extra-warm glow. Small silk or dried fall flowers can be glued into the swag, if more color is desired. Miniature faux pumpkins would add fall flair to this arrangement!

rain forest square

Hues of green and varying leaf textures combine with the scent of caspia and eucalyptus to remind us of the rain forest. There is such diversity of plants in our wondrous world!

What You'll Need

Water mister
Garden clippers
Bunch green eucalyptus
Bunch preserved oak leaves
Bunch seteria
Bunch caspia
Bunch lemon leaves
Bunch boxwood
Bunch integrafolia
Bunch bracken fern
Bunch plumosa fern
Bag old man's beard
Square wreath form
Paddle floral wire, 24 gauge
Hot glue gun, glue sticks
2 freeze-dried white roses

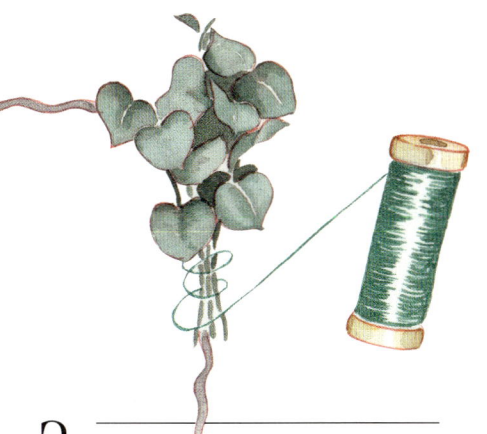

3. Make a small bouquet with 4 to 6 pieces of same plant. Place stems over where wire is attached to wreath. Wrap stems 3 times, moving down length of stems. At last wrap, you will be ½ inch from end of stems. Make sure wire holds stems snugly.

5. To add last bouquet, cut off end ½ inch of stems. Gently lift first bouquet, and slide last bouquet under it. Wrap stems of last bouquet 3 times to hold in place, but as you wrap, leave second wrap loose enough to pull paddle wire under so you can tie off and secure last bunch. Cut wire, leaving a tail of 4 inches. Wrap wire around wreath form to secure.

1. Mist all materials, and cut leaves to varying lengths between 4 and 6 inches long.

2. Attach wire to wreath by wrapping it once around wreath and twisting it on back to secure, beginning at a corner of wreath. (Do not cut wire.)

4. Make another bouquet as before using a different plant. Place this bouquet on top of stems of first bouquet. As you wrap wire, the first wrap will hold last ½ inch of first bouquet as well as top of stems of second bouquet. Continue making same size bouquets and adding them to wreath. At corners, turn bunches to follow wreath form. You will need to add about 20 bouquets to cover wreath.

6. Cut a 4-inch piece of wire for a hanger. Twist wire on back of wreath to form hanger. Glue roses at bottom right corner

candy-coated christmas

You will see visions of sugarplums dancing in your head when you make this sparkling holiday wreath. Assorted miniature fruit, berries, and minty candy canes glisten with a "candy coating" of diamond dust. This evergreen wreath will bring out the child in all of us.

What You'll Need

Small artist paintbrush
White craft glue
Diamond dust or opalescent glitter
54 pieces artificial fruit on wire picks
2 stems red berries
2 dozen plastic candy canes
Artificial pine wreath, 14 inches
Hot glue gun, glue sticks

1. With small artist's paintbrush, coat each piece of fruit with glue. Sprinkle diamond dust over fruit pieces. Repeat process on berries and candy canes. Let dry overnight.

2. Shape evergreen wreath by pulling out and fluffing branches.

3. Twist 3 pieces of different fruit together into a cluster. Place fruit clusters into wreath. Twist stems of fruit into branches. Continue around wreath until it is full.

4. Cut each berry stem into 5 or so pieces; each piece should have about 5 berries. Glue berry stems into wreath. Spread berries throughout wreath.

5. Glue candy canes into wreath at an angle so they stick out from fruits and berries.

Tip
When you store your wreath from year to year, some of the diamond dust might come off. You can easily touch up the wreath by brushing the pieces of fruit with a little more glue and adding a fresh sprinkling of diamond dust.

Variation
For a variation, add a bow to this sparkling confection. Choose a soft color for the ribbon so you don't distract from the pastels of the fruit. A small bow with a few streamers tied at the bottom would look best.

autumn berry candle rings

Warm a cool fall evening with these cozy candle rings. Plump autumn berries in brilliant fall tones encircle orange pillar candles. Perfect as a table centerpiece, the berry rings can also hang on a door as a colorful and bright holiday wreath arrangement.

What You'll Need

Floral wire, 24 gauge
Brown or dark green floral tape
Wire cutters
8 stems orange berry sprays with leaves
3 pillar candles, two 3×6 inches and one 6×6 inches

1. Wrap floral wire with floral tape. Twist tape tightly around wire, and cut wire into 6-inch pieces.

2. Choose berry stems that have sprays of berries instead of clusters. The spray portion should be at least 8 to 12 inches long. Cut off stem end of sprays.

3. Form a berry spray around a 3×6 candle by bending the spray in a ring.

4. Using pieces of taped floral wire, wire 2 berry sprays together to form a ring. Tie berry sprays as tightly together as possible. Wire 6 to 8 places around ring to hold securely.

5. Bend all berries up to form a flat side so ring sits evenly. Keep all berries going in same direction. Repeat for second small ring.

6. Repeat process with remaining berry sprays around larger candle. Wire in as many extra berries as needed to get a full, round shape. Place larger candle and ring in center of the table, with smaller candles and rings on either side.

Tips

These delightful candle rings are perfect around all different sizes of candles. They can even be used around glass hurricanes. The size of the candle will determine the size of the ring you will need.

The trick is to keep the ring as tight and full of berries as possible. Some berry sprays are available with tiny leaves and stems. Others are just berries. Experiment with different types of sprays. When tiny berries are grouped together, they create a cozy glow for fall entertaining.

birdhouse bounty

Create a bird sanctuary at your own back door! Each time you see this wreath, you'll know that spring is on its way.

What You'll Need

Grapevine wreath, 18 inches
Brown chenille stem
Hot glue gun, glue sticks
3 birdhouses on dowels, various shapes
Paint for birdhouses, colors to suit your taste
Paintbrushes
3-inch bird's nest
Ivy bush
Wire cutters
15 to 20 spring flowers
3 small bird eggs
Small bird
Raffia ribbon
Floral wire, 24 gauge

1. Twist chenille stem onto a few strands of grapevine on back of wreath. Make a loop with stem for hanging. Glue chenille stem to hold securely.

2. Paint birdhouses and dowels however you like. Let paint dry completely.

3. Insert birdhouse dowels into bottom center of wreath, leaving space for nest. Glue birdhouses into place. Place nest in front of houses, and glue in place.

4. Cut ivy strands from bush. Wire ivy strands to wreath, beginning at left of birdhouses and going around and up right side of wreath. Let 3 or 4 ivy strands hang 8 to 10 inches below bottom of wreath.

5. Glue flowers around wreath, making a pleasing arrangement. Be sure some flowers hang down. Also, glue 1 or 2 flowers up right side of wreath. Glue bird eggs inside nest and bird to side of nest.

6. With about 8 to 10 strands of raffia, tie a large bow. Cut a piece of floral wire, and twist it around the middle of bow. Wire bow below nest.

holiday pear garland

Faux green pears trim a permanent garland of assorted greenery, berries, natural birch twigs, and golden holly leaves. Place this garland over a doorway, let it cascade down a staircase, or use it to adorn the table. This cheerful garland will help you celebrate the festive Thanksgiving and Christmas seasons.

What You'll Need

36 faux pears
Stem floral wire, 22 gauge
Wire cutters
Brown floral tape
8 green berry stems
5 silk lemon leaf stems
2 pine sprays with gold glitter
Natural birch branches
9-foot silk pine garland
Hot glue gun, glue sticks
2 gold holly sprays

1. Cut floral wire into 6-inch lengths. Extend stem ends of pears with floral wire by covering wire and stem with brown floral tape. Set aside. Cut berry stems, lemon leaf stems, and pine sprays into 4- to 5-inch pieces. Set aside.

2. Place birch branches in pine garland, and twist pine branches around birch to hold in place. Use floral wire if needed for extra security. Birch branches should extend 4 to 5 inches from pine garland.

3. Use floral wire to add berry sprays, pine sprays, and lemon leaf sprays to garland.

4. Add pears by twisting stem ends into garland. Add extra branches, berries, and other leaves as needed to give garland a full and lush look.

5. Cut holly sprays into small pieces, and glue into garland. Use them to hide any wire that shows.

Variations

For a novel approach, add feathered partridges to remind guests of the 12 days of Christmas. Tuck in ribbons or small bows for added texture and color. Make place cards to coordinate a party theme. Cut a small slit into the top of a faux pear, and tuck in a small card with a guest's name on it. Make one for each dinner guest!

high style fall

Go for the unusual! This eye-catching fall wreath works well in a more modern room décor.

What You'll Need

Sweet huck wreath
Brown chenille stem
Hot glue gun, glue sticks
4 berry branches,
16 to 18 inches long
3 flat mushrooms
3 lotus pods
7 pheasant feathers
2 pinecones
2 twigs
10 to 15 silk leaves

1. Twist chenille stem on back of wreath to form a hook for hanging. Glue in place.

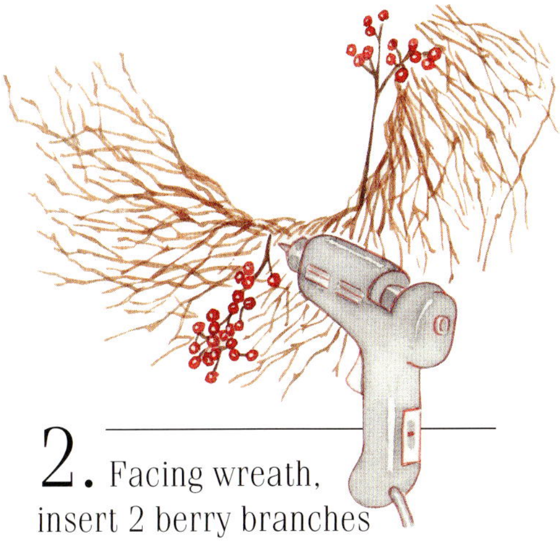

2. Facing wreath, insert 2 berry branches in the 5 o'clock position. Berries should face up and slightly to the right. Insert third and fourth berry branches in same 5 o'clock position, but pointed down and slightly to the left. Glue in place.

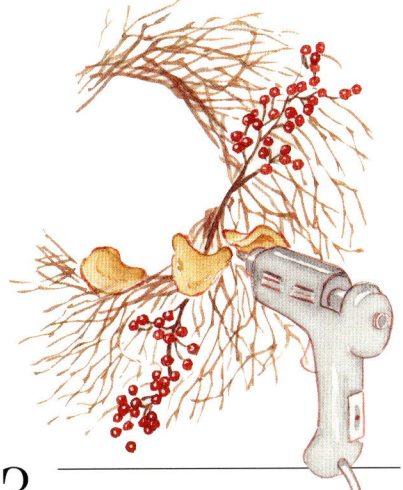

3. In the same area where you placed berries, insert mushrooms at slightly different levels, leaving a slight space between each.

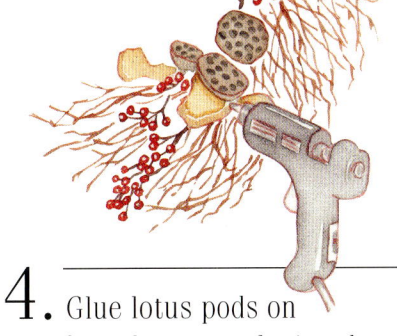

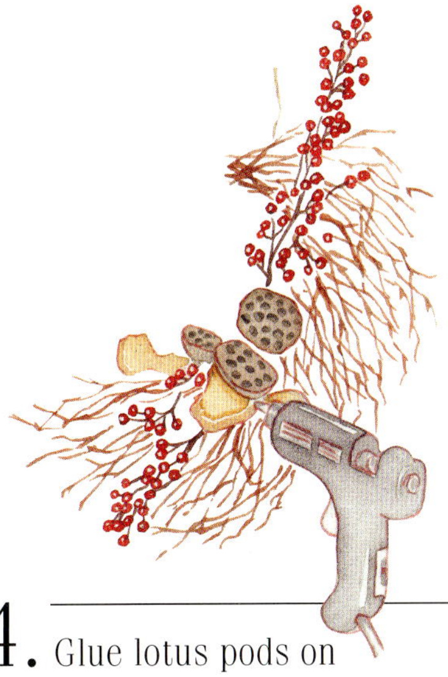

4. Glue lotus pods on top of mushrooms, placing them in a stair-step pattern.

5. Insert and glue feathers, 3 up and 4 down, at the 5 o'clock position. Fan feathers out slightly. Glue pinecones below mushrooms.

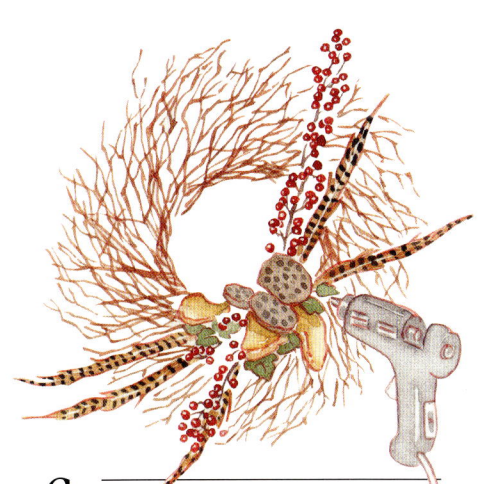

6. Place short twig behind lotus pods pointing into middle of wreath and longer twig hanging down below wreath. Glue leaves below mushrooms and around lotus pods.

sunflower garden

Bright and cheerful silk sunflowers are the focal point of this colorful country garden wreath. Tiny berries and other blossoms seem to sprout among the sunflowers. Let the warm, sunny tones evoke a cozy feeling in your home.

What You'll Need

Wire cutters
3 stems yellow sunflowers
3 stems rust sunflowers
2 stems yellow silk poppies
2 stems chrysanthemums
2 stems permanent bittersweet
Grapevine wreath, 14 inches
Hot glue gun, glue sticks

1. Cut sunflower stems to approximately 1 to 2 inches. Cut apart poppy and chrysanthemum stems, and trim individual flower stems to about 5 inches. Cut off all remaining leaves from sunflowers and save.

2. Cut bittersweet into separate stems. Insert bittersweet stems into wreath. Wrap and bend stems around wreath.

3. Insert poppies into wreath between bittersweet. Space them evenly around wreath. Repeat this process with chrysanthemums, leaving open spaces for sunflowers. Add hot glue to flower stem ends to keep them secure.

4. Glue heads of yellow sunflowers into wreath. Put hot glue gun on backside of sunflower, and push flower into wreath. Form a triangular pattern with yellow flowers first, and then glue on 3 rust sunflowers between them. Keep heads of flowers as flat as possible.

5. Glue individual leaves around sunflowers to hide any glue.

Variations

This wreath can also be used as a candle ring around a glass hurricane. Any variety of country-style silk flowers can be used to complement the sunflowers. The best choices would be any flowers that are smaller than the sunflowers. For a brighter wreath, use only yellow sunflowers. A bow made of ribbon or raffia can also be added if desired. A country print ribbon, such as gingham, would enhance the quaint country charm of this wreath.

autumn splendor

Welcome guests into your home this autumn with an easy-to-create design. Silk fall leaves and mums combined with permanent grasses and a mushroom bird are hot-glued onto an oval grapevine wreath. This simple project is sure to delight family and friends.

What You'll Need

Oval grapevine or twig wreath, 18 inches

1 stem fall leaves, with 3 branches (berries optional)

Wire cutters

Hot glue gun, glue sticks

3 fall-colored silk mums, 3 to 3½ inches wide

2 dried shelf mushrooms with stems, about 5 inches wide

2 stems miniature silk sunflowers

3 clusters permanent grass (fall tones)

3 pieces green silk English ivy, 6 inches long each

3½-inch mushroom bird

Spanish moss

18-inch length covered floral wire, 20 or 22 gauge

Pencil or pen

1. Lay wreath flat. Cut fall leaves into 3 sections, with 1 piece longer than others. Glue long piece into wreath at lower left side extending up left. Glue next piece extending from right side and down. Third piece is glued between other two and extends to lower left.

2. Glue mums in a triangular arrangement, so leaves meet at bottom of wreath. Stagger mums so they are at different heights.

3. Cut mushroom stems about 1 inch long; insert and glue into wreath below mums.

4. Glue miniature sunflowers 1 above the other to left of mums, extending up left side and blending with fall leaves.

5. Glue grass clusters to wreath. Place 1 in center between mums and 1 below each of other 2 mums.

6. Glue 1 piece ivy to upper right of mums, 1 to lower left of mums, and 1 between lower 2 mums.

7. Glue mushroom bird in center of mums, just above grass cluster. Dot glue around bird, and form Spanish moss around base of bird to look like a nest. Do not glue moss in first; bird will not set securely if moss is underneath.

8. Hold wreath at top to balance, and find where hanger should be placed. Work covered floral wire through top of wreath and twist twice at back. Cross wire over itself to make a loop. Twist twice more. Curl ends of wire around a pencil or pen to look like grapevine tendrils.

47

rose hydrangea

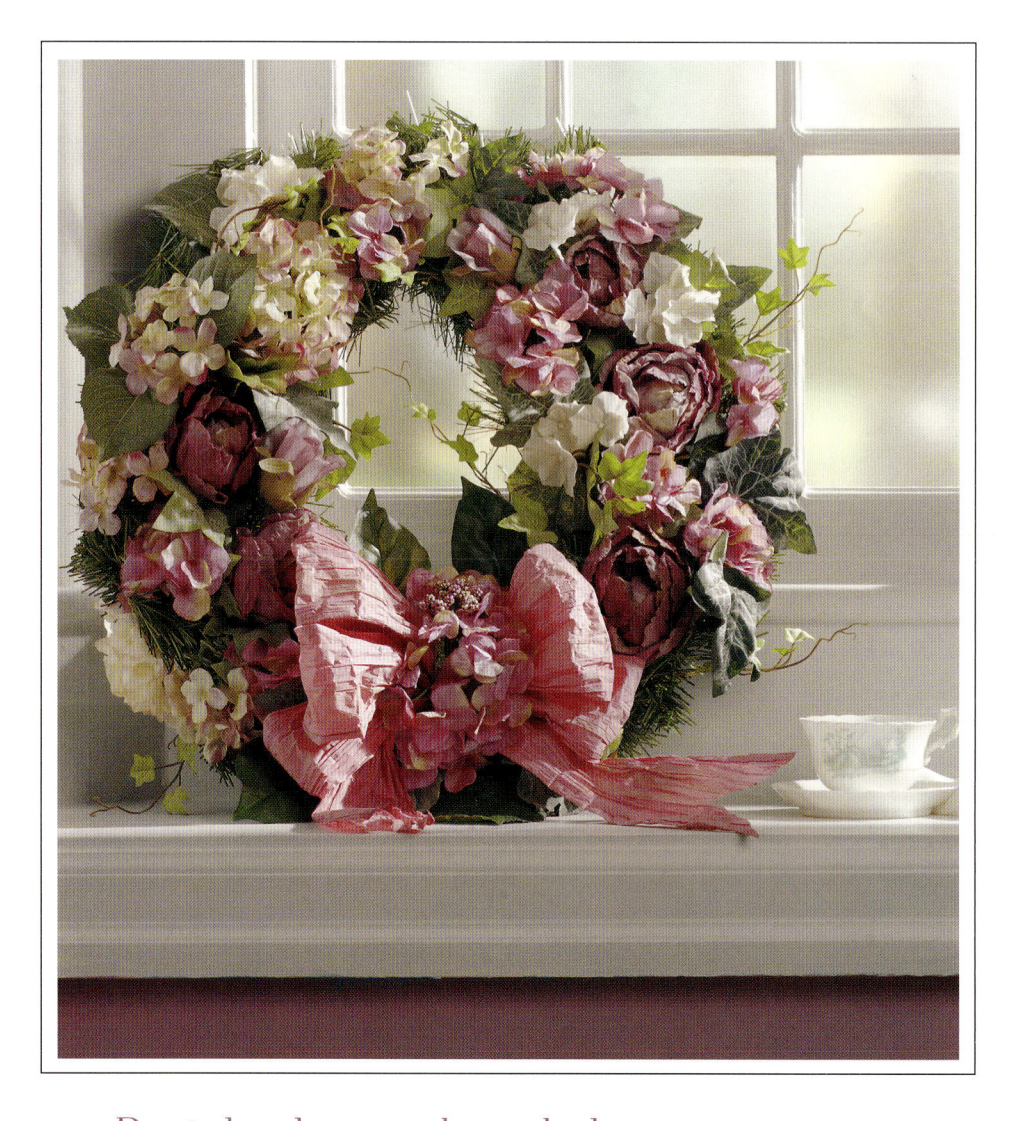

Pastel colors and symbols of love and romance all come together in this beautiful arrangement. Add a touch of elegance to your house with this special wreath.

What You'll Need

Evergreen wreath
Brown chenille stem
Hot glue gun, glue sticks
Ivy bush or swag at least 36 inches long
Heavy-duty craft scissors
5 large red silk roses
3 silk rosebuds
6 silk hydrangea clusters, white and pink
5 silk magnolia leaves, 4 to 5 inches each
2 yards pink paper ribbon
Floral wire, 24 gauge
Wire cutters

1. Fluff wreath by arranging branches. Twist chenille stem on back of wreath to form a hook for hanging. Glue to secure.

2. Cut ivy into sections, and place around wreath, covering about 80 percent of front of wreath. Weave ivy in and out of branches. Spot glue ivy in place.

3. Glue 2 open roses at left side of wreath at about the 7 and 8 o'clock positions. Glue 3 open roses to right side, spacing them at the 2, 3, and 4 o'clock positions. Leave bottom middle of wreath open for bow.

4. Glue 2 rosebuds above large roses on left going up wreath. Glue a rosebud between and to right of large roses on right.

5. Glue a hydrangea cluster at bottom center of wreath. Glue 2 hydrangea clusters between large roses on left. Glue a hydrangea cluster between bottom 2 large roses on right. Cut remaining hydrangeas into pieces, and glue clusters randomly around entire wreath.

6. Glue 5 magnolia leaves to bottom of wreath so they fan around hydrangea blossom. Be sure fan is large enough so that when bow is placed, it does not completely cover the leaves.

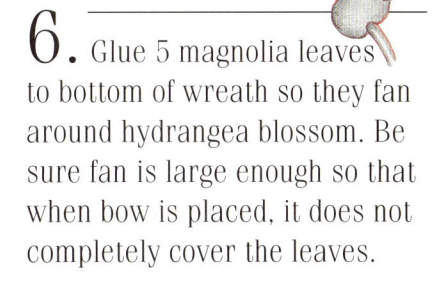

7. Make a 6-loop bow with paper ribbon and floral wire. Wire bow to wreath just under bottom center hydrangea blossom. Cut bow ends in a V.

four calling birds

Four snowy birds call out a message of good will to all. Birch branches trimmed with holly and tiny blossoms form a unique wreath. It looks like this frosty foursome has made a charming wreath their new home for the holidays!

What You'll Need

Stem floral wire, 22 gauge
Brown floral tape
Birch branches, about 24 inches in length (between 140 and 170 branches)
4 matching birds
Hot glue gun, glue sticks
Spanish moss
2 stems silk holly
2 stems white silk miniature roses
Miniature pinecones
Small artist's paintbrush
Craft glue
Diamond dust or opalescent glitter

1. Wrap floral wire with brown floral tape. Separate branches into 4 bundles with about 36 thin branch pieces in each and another 2 bundles with 10 to 15 branches each.

2. With taped wire, tie each bundle in the middle, then tie bundles on each end. Add extra branches as needed to make solid bundles.

3. Make a square with 4 large bundles, and wrap the ends together with wire. The square should measure about 18×18 inches. Leave a few light branches longer at corners to soften wreath. Trim remaining branches so the wreath has a flat back for hanging.

4. Wire 2 smaller bundles to back of wreath to form 4 equal center squares. Again, wire in the middle of the 2 bundles and at either end for good support. Slip in extra branches as needed to strengthen squares.

5. Glue birds in place. They should sit firmly in middle bottom of each center square. Tilt birds forward so wreath still has a flat back. Glue small amounts of Spanish moss at base of each bird to resemble a nest.

6. Cut individual leaves and berries from holly. Glue into place around nest and to hide wire on wreath. Glue on roses. Glue pinecones between holly leaves and flowers.

7. Using a small artist's paintbrush, brush tips of flowers, cones, and holly leaves lightly with glue. Sprinkle with diamond dust. If desired, sprinkle diamond dust on the birds' feathers also. Let dry overnight.

summer eucalyptus

The coming of summer is brought forth in this wreath with its warm pastels and earthy scents of preserved eucalyptus, hydrangea, and plumosa fern. It promises the full burst of summer color that's to come.

What You'll Need

Water mister
1 pound preserved green jade eucalyptus
45 to 50 tips leafless twigs, 18 inches long
Garden clippers
Round wire wreath form, 8 inches
Paddle floral wire, 24 gauge
Wire cutters
3 inches ribbon, 1/8 inch wide
Bunch dried dark green plumosa fern
Bunch dried baby's breath
Bunch dried white gomphrena
Bunch dried purple/blue statice
10 cream strawflowers
1 head seafoam-green dried hydrangea, cut in pieces
Hot glue gun, glue sticks

1. Mist all plants, and cut eucalyptus stems and twigs in varying lengths between 3 and 9 inches.

2. Attach wire by wrapping it once around wreath form and twisting it on back to secure. (Do not cut wire.)

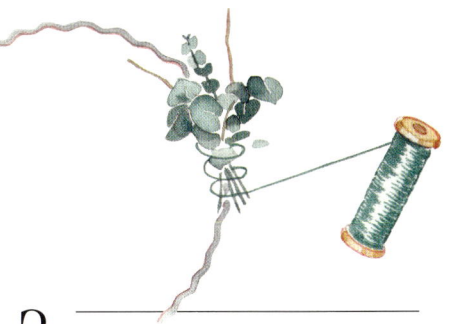

3. Make a small bunch of 4 to 6 stems of eucalyptus and 4 or 5 twigs. Place stems of bunch over where wire is attached to wreath. Wrap stems 3 times, moving down the length of stems with each wrap. At last wrap, you will be 1/2 inch from end of stems. Make sure wire holds stems snugly but not so tightly that they are crushed.

4. Make another bunch as before. Place this on top of stems of first bunch. As you wrap, the first wrap will hold last 1/2 inch of first bunch as well as top of stems of second bunch. Continue making same size bunches and adding them to wreath. You will need to add about 10 bunches to cover wreath.

5. To add last bunch, cut off end 1/2 inch of stems. Gently lift first bunch placed on wreath, and slide last bunch under it. Wrap stems of last bunch 3 times to hold it in place, but as you wrap, leave second wrap loose enough to pull paddle under so you can tie off and secure wire. Cut wire, leaving a tail of 4 inches. Wrap wire around wreath form to secure. Slide wire end under ties and between stems.

6. Cut a 4-inch piece of wire for a hanger. Wrap it around the back of the wreath, making a loop for hanging. Tie ribbon to hanger so you can find it later.

7. Hang wreath. Use glue gun to place florals and ferns evenly throughout wreath.

53

halloween spooktacular

Spooky ghosts frolic with creepy black spiders and orange pumpkins on this wreath of crisp fall leaves. Hang it on your front door so these frightful fellows can tell trick-or-treaters, "Have a Happy Halloween!"

What You'll Need

White tissue paper
Ruler
Scissors
6 white foam balls, 2 inches each
Raffia
Black fine-point felt-tip pen
Hot glue gun, glue sticks
Glass jar, with bottom at least 5 to 6 inches in diameter
Water mister
Paper towels
10 to 12 birch branches, 7 to 8 inches long
Natural grapevine wreath, 18 inches
Bunch dried fall leaves
3 medium artificial pumpkins
12 small artificial pumpkins
10 small black plastic spiders

1. Cut tissue paper into 15×15-inch square pieces; make 6 squares. Place a foam ball in center of paper, and gather paper over ball. Smooth tissue over ball to form head of ghost. Tie tissue under ball with raffia. With pen, draw eyes, nose, and mouth.

2. With glue gun, "draw" a spiderweb shape on bottom of glass jar. The diameter of the web should be 4 to 5 inches. Spray with water, and let glue dry for 1 to 2 minutes. Carefully peel off web. Pat dry with paper towel. Make 3 to 5 webs. Color backs of webs with black pen.

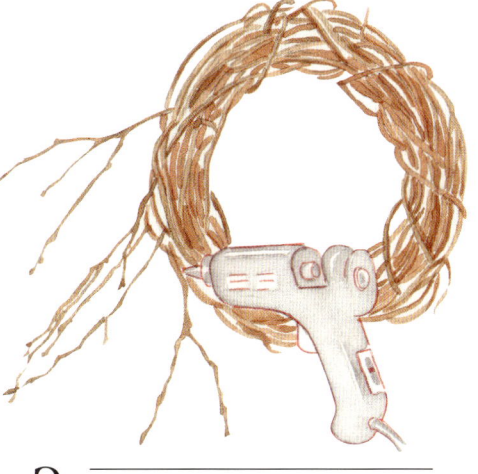

3. Glue pieces of birch branches into grapevine wreath. Be sure to keep branches going in same direction around wreath.

4. Glue dried leaves onto wreath. Again, make sure they go around wreath in same direction.

5. Glue ghosts to wreath. Make sure all the ghosts are facing front. Glue in extra dried leaves as needed.

6. Glue pumpkins between ghosts. Add extra leaves and branches as needed to hold pumpkins in place and to hide glue.

7. Slip spiderwebs over branches. Use small amount of hot glue to secure them to branches. Hot glue spiders around wreath.

new england holiday

Make your New England holiday wreath and garland a family activity. Bring your clippers and spend half an hour collecting 25 pounds of evergreen tips. Be sure to bring along the hot chocolate!

What You'll Need

25 pounds evergreen tips
Garden clippers
Paddle floral wire, 22 gauge
Wire wreath form, 12 inches
Hot glue gun, glue sticks
9 pinecones
2 bunches faux red berries
3 dried orange slices
Red bow with 6 inch tails
12 inches green hemp or jute twine

1. To make wreath: Cut greenery 5 to 9 inches long. Wrap wire around wreath ring, and twist it on back to secure. (Do not cut wire.)

2. Make a small bouquet of 4 to 6 pieces of evergreen. Place stems over wire where it is attached to wreath. Wrap stems 3 times, moving down length of stems with each wrap. At last wrap, you will be ½ inch from end of stems. Make sure wire holds stems snugly but not so tightly that they are crushed. (Note: Balsam fir has a brighter green on side that faces sun. As you make bunches, make certain colors match.)

3. Make another bouquet as before. Place this on top of stems of first bouquet. As you wrap, first wrap will hold last ½ inch of first bouquet as well as top of stems of second bouquet. Continue making bouquets and adding them to wreath. You will need to add about 40 bunches to cover wreath.

4. To add last bunch, cut off end ½ inch of stems. Gently lift first bouquet, and slide last one under it. Wrap stems of last bunch 3 times to hold in place, but as you wrap, leave second wrap loose enough to pull paddle under so you can tie off and secure last bunch. Cut wire, leaving a tail of 10 inches of wire. Wrap wire around last bunches placed, and then make a loop for a hanger.

Tip
For an illuminating decorative touch, weave small Christmas lights throughout the swag.

5. Glue pinecones, berries, and orange slices throughout wreath. Cut a length of wire and wrap it around center of bow. Wire bow to wreath.

6. To make swag: Cut a piece of green jute 15 feet 6 inches long. Make hanging loops at both ends of jute. Twist wire around jute to secure.

7. Make a bouquet with 4 to 5 pieces of greenery, and wire them to jute. Continue making and wiring evergreen bunches to jute until you reach the end. Use shorter branches at end of swag to cover stems. Wrap wire around last few bouquets 5 times. Cut wire 4 inches from last twist, and slide wire under twists.

victorian valentine heart

A satin- and lace-covered heart is entwined with old-fashioned garden roses, wisteria, and dainty sweet peas. Romantic ribbons and sprays of pearls evoke a Victorian charm, which makes this wreath a perfect choice to give to your valentine.

What You'll Need

Heart-shaped foam wreath
Satin ribbon, ¾ inch wide
Hot glue gun, glue sticks
Pearl-headed corsage pins
Lace ribbon
Wire cutters
6 open roses
2 stems spray roses
Stem rose vine
Stem wisteria
2 stems sweet pea
Pearl sprays
Pearl garland
Sheer ribbon

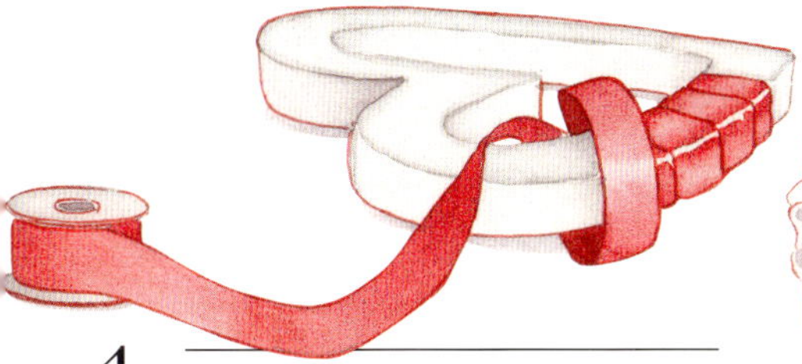

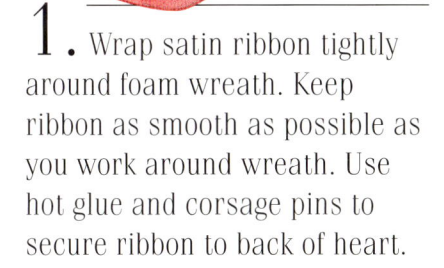

1. Wrap satin ribbon tightly around foam wreath. Keep ribbon as smooth as possible as you work around wreath. Use hot glue and corsage pins to secure ribbon to back of heart.

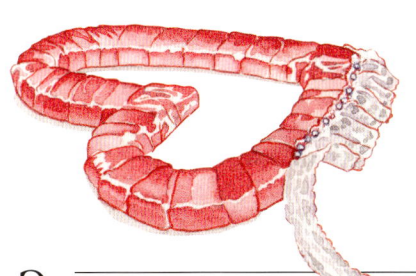

2. On back of wreath, use corsage pins to secure lace. Pleat ribbon as you pin it down, forming a ruffle. Continue all around wreath.

3. Trim rose stems. Hot glue roses to top and bottom Vs of heart. Use corsage pins as needed to add remaining flowers. Glue large flowers first, then add smaller ones. Let a purple sweet pea spray hang down from wreath bottom. Add leaves to hide excess glue.

4. Pin pearl sprays into top cluster of flowers.

5. Pin pearl garland to bottom V of wreath. From the shear ribbon, make a large cluster of loops and long streamers, pinning cluster together with a corsage pin. Pin ribbon cluster to bottom V of wreath, letting pearls and ribbon cascade together. Tie a few rose buds to ends of streamers to form love knots.

6. Glue or pin in extra blossoms and leaves where needed to hide excess glue.

Tips and Variations

Any number of combinations of materials can be used for this wreath. The ribbons and silk flowers can be changed to whatever you can find. Any shade of pink, rose, and mauve works well. Keep the flower choices to old-fashioned varieties such as roses or even lilies of the valley. Keep the ribbon clusters thin and delicate so the flowers really stand out.

williamsburg medallion

Classic elegance is reflected in this Williamsburg-style medallion wreath. It's wonderful for the holidays, but it can decorate your house all winter long!

What You'll Need

Wicker paper plate holder
Green chenille stem
Hot glue gun, glue sticks
23 magnolia leaves with stems, 4 to 6 inches each
Small artificial evergreen wreath, candle-ring size
Lotus pod
4 large pears, 3 inches each
8 red pomegranates, 1 inch each
4 small pears, 1 to 2 inches each
8 red cherries, 1 inch each
Floral wire, 24 gauge
Wire cutters
Scissors
Two 18-inch lengths gold cording

1. Twist chenille stem into loop; place on front (concave side) of wicker plate holder. Glue in place. On back of plate holder, glue 4 large magnolia leaves, equally spaced around plate, stems facing center of plate. Leave a 4-inch gap in center of plate holder. Half of each leaf will hang off plate holder.

2. Glue 2 magnolia leaves between each of 4 leaves already placed, still leaving center of plate holder empty.

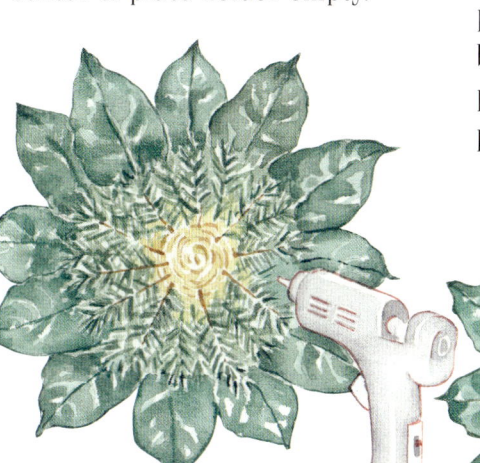

3. Glue candle-ring wreath to center of plate holder, covering leaf stems.

4. Glue lotus pod to center of candle-ring wreath. Pull wreath branches up to support pod and to add depth.

5. Glue 4 large pears around lotus pod, leaving 1 inch between pears and pod. Glue 2 pomegranates in spaces between pears. Glue a small pear outside each group of pomegranates.

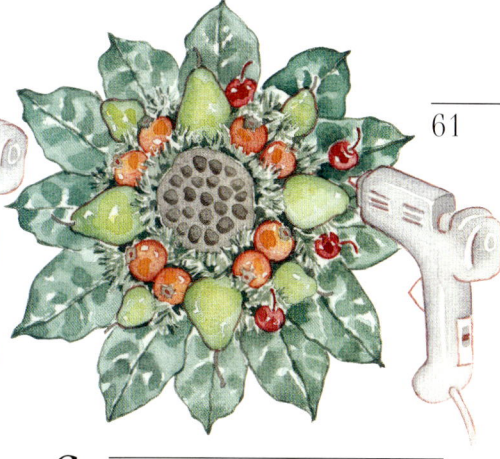

6. Glue cherries on either side of large pears. Overlap and glue 8 smaller leaves around perimeter of fruit. Glue 3 large magnolia leaves at bottom so they hang lower than first leaves.

7. Make 2 separate 6-inch loops with gold cording, and glue loops below lotus pod; let extra cord hang down. Tie a knot 2 inches from end of each cord tail. Unravel ends.

stars and stripes forever

Show your patriotic spirit when you display this wreath on your front door. Blue and silver star cutouts and red and white silk flowers unite for a Fourth of July tribute—or display your colors all year long!

WHAT YOU'LL NEED

White paper
Pen
Scissors
Cardboard
8 blue plastic plates
Small paintbrush
Craft glue
Silver glitter
Round foam wreath
Red, white, and blue striped ribbon
Hot glue gun, glue sticks
Straight pins
Wire cutter
6 stems red silk gerbera daisies
2 stems white silk pom pon mums
Stapler, staples
Silver star garland

1. Trace star pattern from page 64 onto white paper, and cut out. Trace star onto cardboard, and cut out. Trace star onto center of a plate. Cut out. Make 8 stars.

2. With paintbrush and glue, brush a stripe of glue around edges of stars. Sprinkle with silver glitter. Let dry completely (at least 3 hours).

3. Wrap striped ribbon around wreath. Keep color stripes uniform. Use hot glue and straight pins to secure ribbon to back of wreath.

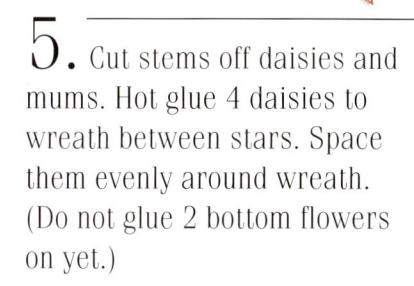

4. Use straight pins to attach 5 stars to wreath, leaving space between stars for silk flowers. (Note: Do not use hot glue on stars; they will melt.) Hide pinhead by placing it where glitter is. Pin in three places around each star to secure.

5. Cut stems off daisies and mums. Hot glue 4 daisies to wreath between stars. Space them evenly around wreath. (Do not glue 2 bottom flowers on yet.)

6. Cut four 6-inch pieces of ribbon. Make ribbon pieces into loops, and pin them to bottom of wreath to resemble a bow. Use hot glue to secure, if needed. Cut 3 streamers into desired lengths.

7. Staple a star to the end of each streamer. Hide staples in glitter.

8. Wrap end of star garland around a straight pin. Pin star garland into wreath and wrap loosely around entire wreath. Secure opposite end of garland with another pin. Hot glue pins in place to secure.

9. Glue bottom daisies over bow middle. Glue mums on either side of daisies, with 1 placed between bottom daisies.

Enlarge pattern 133 percent.

Tips and Variations

Materials for this wreath can change with availability. Keep the size of the stars the same as the silk flowers, so they are both equally important on this wreath. If desired, gold glitter and gold star garland can be used. When adding the star garland to the wreath, keep it loosely wrapped on the wreath. The movement of the tiny stars adds an exciting touch reminiscent of exploding fireworks!

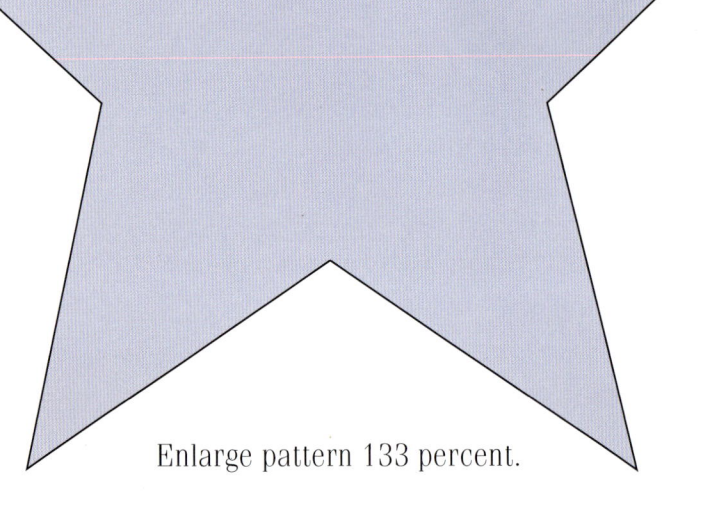